A Very Young Gymnast

Also by Jill Krementz

The Face of South Vietnam
(with text by Dean Brelis)

Sweet Pea—A Black Girl
Growing Up in the Rural South

Words and Their Masters
(with text by Israel Shenker)

A Very Young Dancer

A Very Young Rider

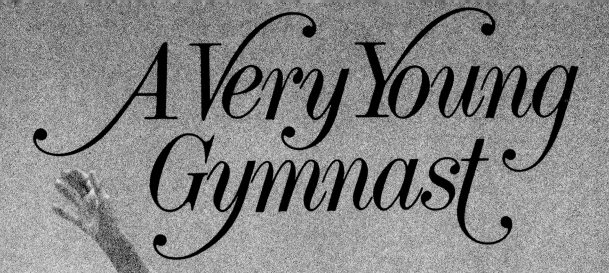

A Very Young Gymnast

Written and Photographed by
Jill Krementz

Alfred A. Knopf
New York, 1978

This is a Borzoi Book
published by Alfred A. Knopf, Inc.
Copyright © 1978 by Jill Krementz
All rights reserved under International and Pan-American Copyright Conventions.
Published in the United States by Alfred A. Knopf, Inc., New York, and
simultaneously in Canada by Random House of Canada Limited, Toronto.
Distributed by Random House, Inc., New York.

Library of Congress Cataloging in Publication Data
Krementz, Jill.
A very young gymnast.
1. Gymnastics for women.   2. Gymnastics for children.   I. Title.
GV464.K74   1978   796.4′1   78-5502
ISBN 0-394-50080-6

Manufactured in the United States of America
First Edition

For
my brother, Tony Kent,
——*with love*——

Gymnastics is so much fun! I've been on the gym team at school ever since I was seven. When I was little, I always used to stand on my head. I'm ten now. My name is Torrance York and I live in New York City.

There are four gymnastic events for girls—vaulting, uneven parallel bars, balance beam, and floor exercise. When you compete, a perfect score would be 10 points in each. Every time you make a mistake, the judges deduct from 10. Most serious faults are half a point off.

My dream is to make the United States Olympic Team. This year I'm going to be in twenty-seven competitions.

Beam is my favorite. The regulation beam is approximately 16 feet long and just under 4 inches wide. It's almost 4 feet above the floor. It seems much higher when you're up there doing acrobatics.

The best way to keep from falling is to hold your body tight and stay centered. Ninety-nine percent of what you do on the beam is maintaining your balance.

In competitions you have to use the entire length of the beam, and your beam routine has to be at least a minute and 15 seconds and no longer than a minute 35. At a minute 30, the judges give you a warning, and at a minute 35 they stop looking. The way you mount and dismount is also very important.

Floor exercises are fun but tiring because you do a lot of fast tumbling on a floor mat that is just under 40 square feet, and you're supposed to use as much of the mat as possible. You do a routine in time to music that has to be at least a minute long but no longer than a minute 30.

Your music has to be a piece played by only one instrument, and it's usually a piano on a phonograph record or tape. Mine is called "Siamese Cat." For the Olympics or international meets they usually have a real piano player.

A good routine shows lightness, strength, speed, height, and rhythm, and it has elements of risk. Years ago the floor ex was done on a wood floor, but too many people got hurt.

I really love the uneven parallel bars too, but it hurts my hands to work on them. The bars are made of wood or fiberglass.

On beam, floor, and bars your different tricks—or moves—are separated into three groups according to how hard they are: superiors, mediums, and basics. You have to do three superiors and four mediums in each of these events.

I like vaulting because it's quick and it's fun.

The horse, which is padded and covered with leather, is the same height as the beam. Medieval knights used to have to vault over a wooden horse. Theirs had a head and tail. But the knights didn't have mats.

My school has the best gym team in New York City. You have to try out in the fall. I made the team in second grade, but now you have to be in the fourth grade. There are sixteen members on the team, and we have competitions against lots of other schools. Every year we have a different team leotard, and this year ours is three shades of blue.

Our coach's name is Annette Asmus. She's from Germany, and she was on the German State Team when she was twenty. She is also a judge for national meets. Her husband, Holger, was on the Junior National Team in Germany. They met in a gymnasium. Sometimes he helps her teach us tumbling and vaulting.

We have gym class three days a week after school from 4:00 to 5:30. We start each class with fifteen minutes of warmups so we won't pull our muscles.

During class we take turns on each piece of equipment. Tumbling takes the most effort for me, so I like to start with it while I still have a lot of strength. I work on things like handstand pirouettes, and I practice my front aerials to get them higher. Aerials are when you turn over in the air without your hands touching the floor.

The tricks by themselves aren't that hard. It's putting them all together into a tumbling pass, which is a series of tricks, that takes all your energy.

In floor ex my hardest tumbling pass is a round-off to a back handspring to a whip back to two back handsprings to a back tuck. A whip back is a quick back handspring without touching the floor with your hands, and a back tuck is when you do a flip while keeping your knees against your chest. You need to have two or three different passes in your routine.

Whenever I learn new tricks for the beam, I start off by doing them on a line on the floor. Then I practice on a low beam between stacked mats, and as I get more confident I take away the mats, one by one. Then I move to the regular beam, and Annette spots me until I'm ready to try it by myself. A spotter is someone who stands near the apparatus and catches you if you fall.

It usually takes me a few weeks to learn a new trick. It takes a little longer to make it stick so that I don't fall off or wobble. My best tricks are a front aerial, a side aerial, and a back tuck. I'm working on a back walkover layout, which is two tricks put together. First you do a back walkover—it's like a backbend except your legs split in the air—and then you go right into a layout, which is a backward somersault in the air with your body and legs straight.

Annette keeps telling me to stretch my body as much as possible for a straight handstand. It's one of the first things we learn, but we have to keep practicing it all the time.

Turns are important on beam, and it helps a lot if you grab the beam with your toes. The secret of good turning is to turn everything at once. Every time you lift a leg forward, you have to keep your hips back. If your hips are square and your stomach is in, when you go for a jump you'll be properly centered.

Before you vault, you have to position your vaulting board. I like mine to be six of *my* feet—4 regular feet—away from the horse. It's very important for it to be straight, because a crooked board throws me off center.

The approach is very important too. You have to keep your elbows close to your body and move them forward and back to get maximum speed. You should be looking straight ahead so you can see the horse and the board at the same time. You need to be running fast so that you can hit the vaulting board with a lot of force. The best way of increasing your speed is to run on the balls of your feet, not your tippy toes, and to try not to let your heels touch the ground.

The way you hit the board and the way you come off it are both crucial. Your body has to be at a certain angle, depending on which vault you're doing. You try to touch the horse with your hands for as short a time as possible. When you hold on, it's called "riding the horse," and you get deductions for that.

It's important to keep your legs straight and together, your body tight, and your toes pointed.

The after-flight is also very important. That's how high and how far you travel after rebounding off the horse. You should travel at least the length of your body. You land on a mat that is 4 inches thick so you won't hurt yourself. But sometimes you do.

Before working out on the bars, I have to adjust them to my size. The height of the bars can't be changed—just the distance between them, provided it's between 21 and 30 inches. I'm 4 feet 3 inches tall, so my bars are very close together. But someone else who is the same height might want to have the bars set wider apart if she has a longer torso.

Then I chalk my hands to prevent slipping. Sometimes I just use spit. Working on bars really kills your hands. After a while you build up calluses, but they can rip off and *that* hurts. You can use tape or grips, but then you slip even more because you don't have the feel of the bars.

One of the superior moves in my bar routine is casting into a handstand pirouette, so I usually practice that a few times. Since "pirouette" means to turn, you have to be able to switch your grip on the bar while in a handstand position. Your arms are supposed to be very straight and your body very tight. I learned this move in fourth grade.

Sometimes when I get frustrated, I make funny faces—like when I'm learning a new trick, such as a front somie catch between bars. That's when you do a forward somersault off the low bar and catch the high bar. If you don't catch the high bar, you fall on your back.

When the rips on my palms bleed, I cry because it hurts so much. Once in a while I cry because I'm just so tired and nothing seems to go right.

After class it's fun to just fool around. Sometimes we have races climbing up the ropes.

My friend Eve and I practice splits on the beam.

Michelle and I usually have handstand contests.

On Monday nights Michelle, Eve, and I go to the Long Island Turnverein. We go right after team workout, so we have a quick picnic dinner in the school locker room. *Turnverein* means "gymnastics club" in German. Club members are called Turners, and it was the Turners who brought gymnastics to the United States in 1848.

Our instructor is Gene Keller, and we work out for two hours. It's the same as gym class and just gives me a little more practice. It also means that I can enter the Turner competitions.

We have Turner meets three times a year. You have to wear a number on your leotard since there are so many competitors.

Boys compete too. They have six events—vaulting, parallel bars, which are even, high bar, rings, side horse, and floor ex. They don't use music for their floor work because they just tumble and leave out the dance. They use different apparatus because they're stronger. Gymnastics used to be a sport for men only.

On Wednesday and Thursday nights I work with Annette's husband, Holger. He spots me on bars when I'm learning new tricks.

But mostly we work on tumbling because I need someone who's strong enough to catch me in the air—like when I do a back layout full twist. That means keeping your body entirely straight while doing a back somersault in the air and adding a full twist to it at the same time. Holger keeps telling me that my jumps need more height. But he would say that even if I hit the ceiling.

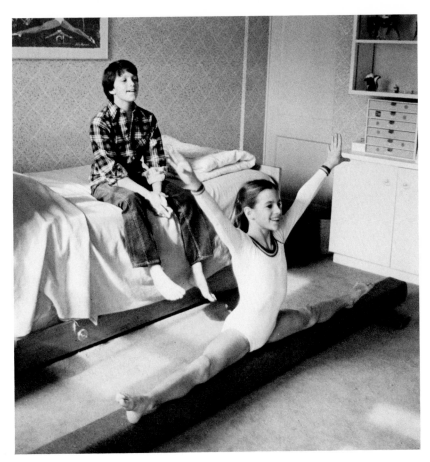

If I'm not too tired when I get home, and if I don't have too much homework, I work on my low beam. Sometimes my brother, Clifton, comes in and watches. Mostly he tells me how bad my form is, and I tell him, "Why don't you try it? It's not as easy as you think."

On Thursday mornings before school I take ballet for an hour with Leigh Welles at her ballet school. We work on flexibility and stretching my muscles so they don't look all clumped up.

We work a lot on arching my back and keeping my stomach flat. Miss Welles makes me practice stretching my arch for my back walkover. She asked me if I knew what a smooth arch looked like and I told her the McDonald's sign, but she said it was better to think of a rainbow.

Another way of smoothing the arch in my back is to do situps. As I go up and down, I have to touch each vertebra to the floor.

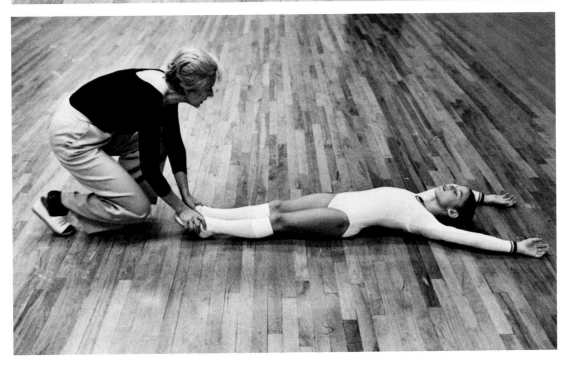

People think that "point your feet" means "point your toes," but what it really means is to arch your feet in a certain way and stretch them.

We also work on various dance positions in front of a mirror, so whenever I land after a leap I can do it in a way that looks nice.

After my lesson I have to rush so I won't miss my first class at regular school.

This year Mom took me to see Dr. Friedman, who is part of the Sports Medicine Program at Lenox Hill Hospital. They take care of a lot of athletes like Pelé and Joe Namath and dancers like Baryshnikov. They also take care of the Knicks, the Rangers, and the Cosmos.

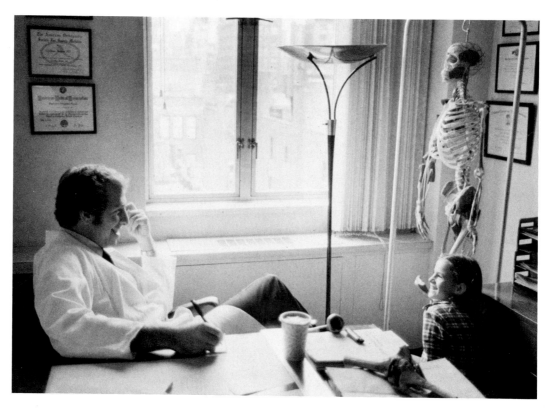

Dr. Friedman has a skeleton in his office, which he calls Ralph, and he told me to show him on Ralph the parts of my body that hurt me. I told him that my left knee hurts when I lock it or stand a certain way.

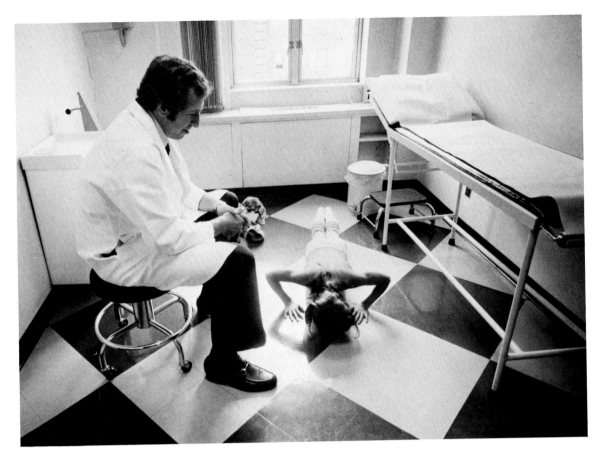

Then he asked me to show him how I warm up so he could examine my joints. He told me I was very flexible.

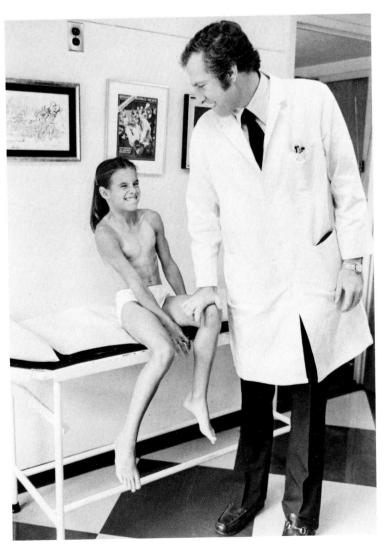

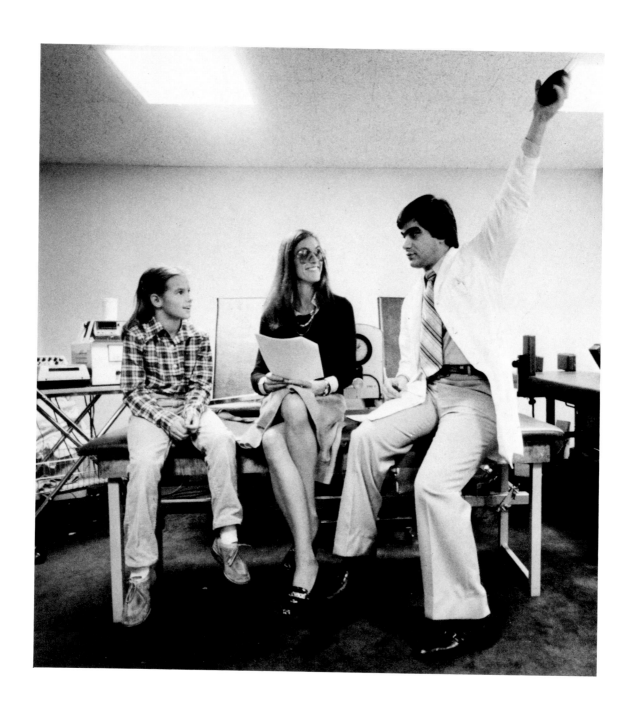

Afterwards he took me next door to the physical therapist, who showed me how to exercise with weights every other day to build up my shoulders, hips, and upper thigh muscles. I'm supposed to hold one weight in my right hand and lift it up and down slowly twenty-five times. Then I do the same with my left hand. I have to strap weights to my ankles and do the same thing, only lying down and with more weight. Lots of gymnasts jump up and down with weights on their ankles, but Dr. Friedman says this is bad for your knees.

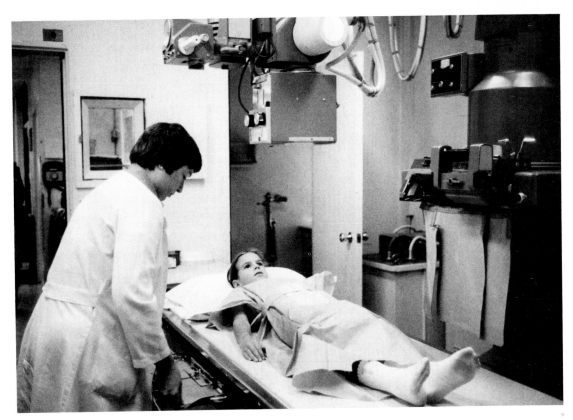

I also got X-rayed so they can have a permanent set of X-rays on hand. Then, if I hurt myself, they can see what my bones used to look like before I damaged them.

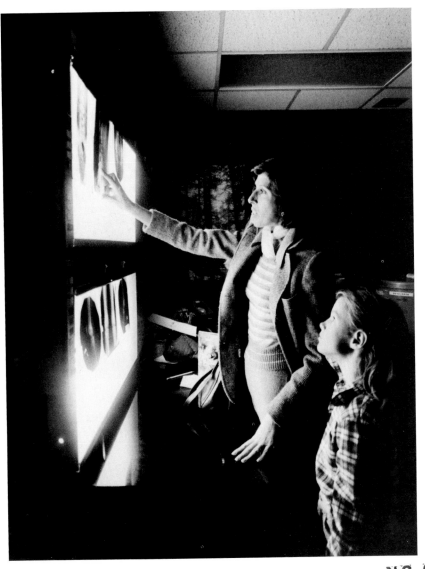

On Friday afternoons we usually have school competitions because that's the day we get out early. Sometimes the competitions are at our school, and sometimes we meet at our opponents' school. I like them better at our gym because I'm used to our equipment.

This year we had four meets, and then in March the five teams with the highest scores competed against each other in the New York City Interschool Championship. It was held at The Horace Mann School.

Our team got the highest number of points, which means we won the trophy. I won the medal for first place all-around in New York City! All-around is the total score of all four events added together.

On Saturdays and Sundays I compete on my own in compulsories and optionals to qualify at my level for State Championships. Most of the meets are at Schnaars Gymnastics Center in Farmingdale, Long Island, which has one of the best gyms.

I always try to look nice when I compete. I get very picky about how my hair looks, and I wear my favorite leotards. My grandmother sews the trim on them. She's my father's mother. My father died when I was five. Grandma always tells me how proud Daddy would be of me now.

My cousin Eliot usually comes along and so does my brother. Clifton works on his homework while we're warming up and when he gets bored. Mom does her homework too, when I'm not performing. She used to be an ambulance driver and a nurse, and now she's getting her master's degree so she can be a family therapist.

There's a panel of judges for each event. Judges have to pass a very difficult test.

In competitions we start with compulsories in all four events. Then we change leotards and do optionals. Compulsories are routines made up by the United States Gymnastics Federation. In optionals you make up your own routines with your own tricks—that's when you do all the hard stuff.

There are four levels—Beginner, which is Class III; Intermediate, which is Class II; Advanced, which is Class I; and Elite, which is the division from which they pick the international teams. I'm in Class I, except when I'm competing in a qualifying meet for the Amateur Athletic Union's Junior Olympics. Then I'm in Class III because of my age.

They give you about an hour and a half to warm up on all the apparatus. I love going to the Gymnastics Center to compete because I get to meet lots of other girls and see what they're doing.

When the warmup time is over, Mrs. Schnaars makes an announcement that the meet is about to begin.

We usually start with vaulting because that's the order in the Olympics—vault, bars, beam, and floor. I wait until it's my turn. I usually feel a little nervous, so I like to sit alone and concentrate on my routines.

At the beginning of each event the head judge signals to start, and I return her signal to show I'm ready. If you start and the judges aren't looking, it's called a false start and you get a zero.

When you vault, each judge writes down a score and the different scores are averaged. Then you vault again and the scoring process is repeated. The highest score of the two vaults is the one that counts.

My optional vault is a handspring full twist.

They have an official timer to time your routine on beam and floor. Your bar routine isn't timed, but it's about 45 seconds.

The judges are *so* strict! Sometimes they take off a tenth of a point if you fiddle with your hair or leotard while you're competing, or if you wobble even a little on beam. They can also deduct for your appearance, like if your underwear shows or if you look too grim.

On beam, bars, and floor the judges also average their scores. But you never get more than one try.

When I competed in Class III compulsories, it was easy for me compared to Class I, which I've been doing for about eight months. For example, on beam you don't have to do a cartwheel, and on vault you only have to do a horizontal squat.

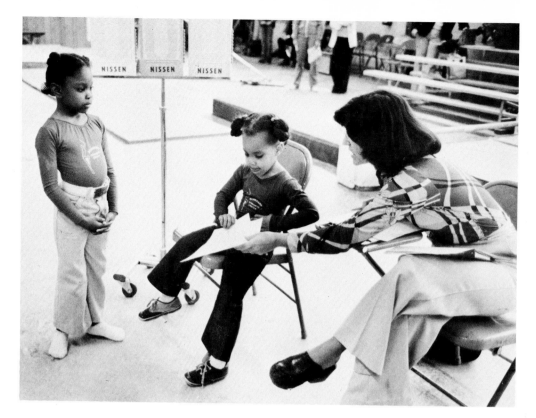

There are always a few little kids who get to run with the judges' scores to the score table, where they are averaged, and then your score is flashed on a special sign after the next girl has finished competing.

They post the scores on a big board. The fifth column is for **A-A**, which is your all-around total—that's the total of your four events. They add your all-around scores for the compulsories and optionals, and that is your final total. You have to get 64 to qualify for State Championships in Class I. It used to be 60.

After the meet is over, they give out the awards. You stand on a podium the same way they do at the Olympics.

When I get home I hang my medals, if I won any, in a special place in my room.

Another big meet that I competed in this year was the Regional Rhythmic Gymnastics Meet. Rhythmic gymnastics originated in West Germany and is just starting to get popular in this country. It's a combination of gymnastics and dance to music with hand apparatus—jump ropes, wooden hoops, balls, ribbons, and Indian clubs. The balls and the clubs are the hardest, so we don't use them yet. A team can have as many members as you want, and there are both individual and group exercises. A group exercise can only have a maximum of six people. There are only two age groups—fourteen and under, and over fourteen.

I like rhythmics but I'm not very good at it. The ribbons are 9½ feet long, and I kept getting tangled up during our practice sessions.

Everything went okay during the meet, and I won third place in the compulsory jump rope. It's harder than it looks because you have to do a lot of tricks like throwing the rope into the air and catching it again, and they take points off when the rope is slack or when there is a loss of rhythm.

The exercise with the ribbon is really pretty. It's made of satin, and you have your choice of a lot of pretty colors. There's one trick where you can make it look like ribbon candy. The main thing is to keep the ribbon in motion.

Gymnastics meets at Madison Square Garden are so exciting. This year I went to the American Cup with Mom and Annette. The American Cup is an international competition, and all of the best gymnasts in the world are invited to compete.

I liked watching our American gymnasts the best. I saw Kathy Johnson, who is on the United States Team, and Donna Turnbow, who is the U.S. All-Around National Champion. Kurt Thomas and Bart Conner are two of our best male gymnasts. They were both on the United States Olympic Team in 1976.

Two other gymnasts that I like a lot were there too—Karen Kelsall and Mitsuo Tsukahara.

Karen is a Canadian who trains in the United States. She made the Olympic Team when she was only thirteen. You're supposed to be fourteen, but she was so good they made an exception.

Tsukahara is from Japan—the Japanese have the best men's gymnastics team in the world. He did an iron cross on the rings and that's really hard. A couple of years ago he invented a vault that Nadia Comaneci later used. You have to do a quarter or a half twist onto the horse and then a one-and-a-half back somersault off it with your body in a tucked, piked, or layout position. Lots of gymnasts do the Tsukahara vault now. I'm just beginning to learn it.

The person I love to watch the *most* is Nadia. This year the Romanian team went on a U.S. tour, and one of their stops was New York. They put on a joint exhibition at the Garden with some of our country's best gymnasts.

I was so excited that I arrived an hour early. Hardly anyone was there except for the gymnasts who were going to perform, and I got to watch them warm up.

Nadia warmed up on the beam first.
A lot of people took pictures but I just looked.

Her coach's name is Bela Karoly, and he spotted her while she warmed up on the uneven parallel bars. She always chalks up her bars and wears grips.

Jackie Cassello, a friend of mine, was there as a member of the American team. She's on our Junior Elite Team, and I used to compete against her at the Schnaars Center when she lived on Long Island. Now she lives in Connecticut because she's training with Muriel Grossfeld. Muriel is a former Olympic gymnast, and she coaches a lot of the top gymnasts in the United States. We talked for a while, and she introduced me to Frank Bare, who is the Executive Director of the U.S. Gymnastics Federation. Jackie's a year older than I am.

I also saw Diana Ross, who brought her daughters, and Cathy Rigby, who was on our Olympic Team in 1968 and 1972. Cathy was really good on beam and won a silver medal in the 1970 World Games, the first medal ever won by an American in international competition. Now she has a gymnastics school in California.

The exhibition began with a parade of teams and the playing of the two anthems. Two of the Americans who performed were Sue Joffe, the national champion in rhythmic gymnastics, and my friend Jackie. Most people performed in one or two events.

Nadia performed in everything. Her technique is really great. It was about the best exhibition I've ever seen.

In March a very exciting thing happened. Annette told us our team had been invited to Germany for two weeks in June to compete against some West German teams. She told us to ask our parents if we could go. Ten of us signed up, plus Ginny Seldon and Lisa Strausburg, who go to schools nearby. Sometimes they work out with our team.

To help pay the expenses for the trip, we all sold raffle tickets at the school fair. They cost twenty-five cents each, and the two winners got gift certificates from Herman's sporting goods store.

Susan, Eve, and I sold lemonade on weekends. We set up a stand in Central Park.

Our first customers gave us a lot of advice. They told us we should use fresh lemons, that we should have plenty of change, and that we should raise our prices. We took some of their advice. We raised our prices.

We spent a lot of time rehearsing a group sequence to exhibit for the West Germans. It's choreographed to the music from *Live and Let Die*, which was Ginny's idea but we all voted. The whole thing takes about three minutes and starts off with all of us in a squatting position. Then we open up like a flower and separate to the corners and edges of the mat.

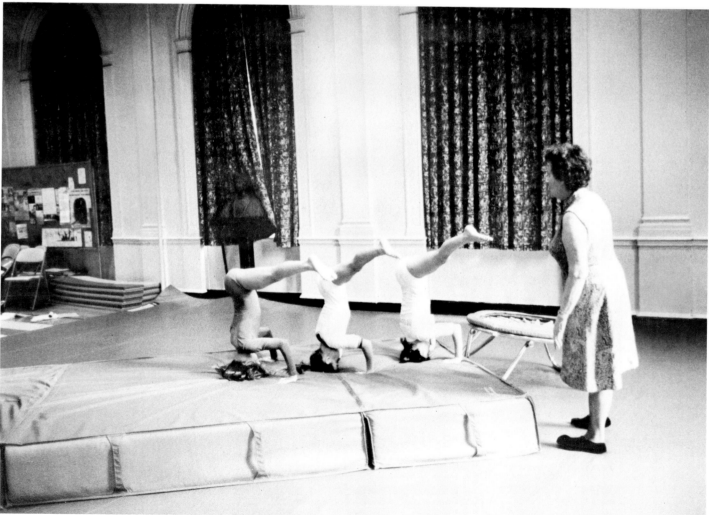

The best part is the end. Ginny does a dive roll off the mini-tramp over Michelle, Eve, and me while we're doing headstands. We practiced this in three stages. The hard part was holding a headstand on such a squishy mat. Miss Duckett, who used to teach gym, coached us.

Annette got us new one-piece warmups that said "New York" across the back. We put American flags on them. Then she gave us instructions on how to act in Germany. She told us that we had to remember not to cross streets on the red light, because you get fined there if you do.

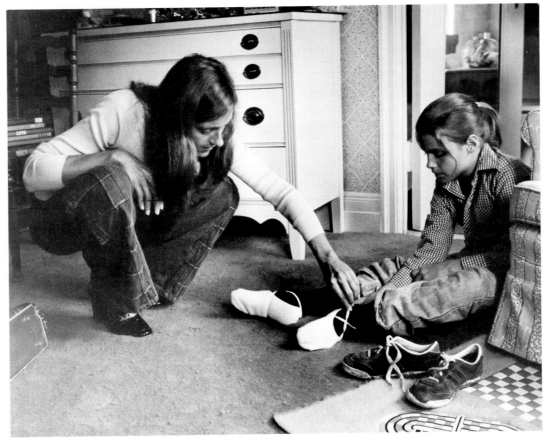

The day before we left, there was a lot to do. Mom helped me put elastics on my new peds, and I bought some hair ribbons at Bloomingdale's.

The best way to pack a duffel bag is to fold and roll all your clothes so they don't get too wrinkled. Mom taught me a neat trick for weighing it. First you weigh yourself, and then you weigh yourself holding the bag and subtract your weight. My duffel came to only 21 pounds. I packed a second small suitcase with games and some school books because I had some summer homework to do.

Finally it was time to leave, and Mom and Clifton came out to the airport to see me off. Mom told me to remember to eat, which I never do when I'm competing, and to get enough sleep.

Then we boarded. I sat next to Susy Kimball.

Our first stop was the little town of Rendsburg. We all stayed with German families. Most of them had daughters our age who were on the Rendsburg team. Whitney stayed with Silke Tittel and her parents, and Ritchey and Eve stayed with the Klemmer family. One of their daughters, Britta, was too young to compete. But their other daughter, Inge, was on the team.

I stayed with Karin Runge, who spoke a little English but not much.

The Rendsburg team held the meet, and a team from Lüneburg was invited, just like us, so that made it a triple meet.

While we were getting dressed, Holger met with the Rendsburg coach. They discussed the rules and regulations for the meet.

We had our own locker room.

We had warmups for about an hour, which was good because we needed to get used to their equipment.

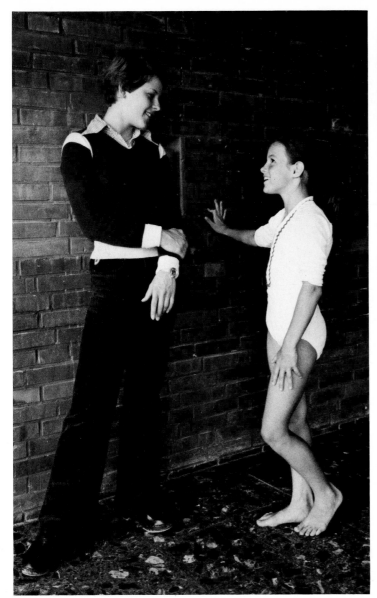 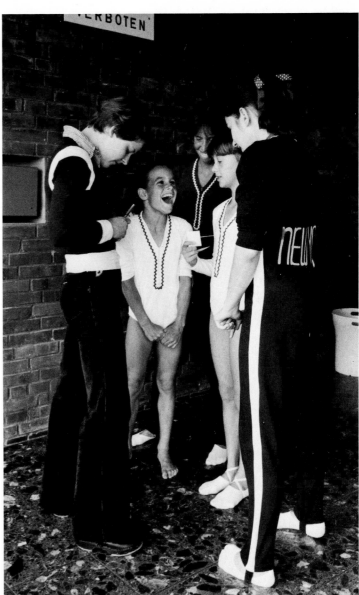

I talked for a while with Andrea Bieger, who is the top-ranked gymnast in West Germany. She went to the 1976 Olympics in Montreal with her team. There were six of them and one alternate. Andrea started doing gymnastics when she was three! We all got her autograph.

At four o'clock it was time to begin. We all marched into the auditorium.

They played different music for each team.

Then we stood under our flags for the national anthems. I felt very proud.

The head judge signaled for the first girl to begin.

The kids from Rendsburg started, and Karin, my German sister, went first.

Like the Olympics, the meet started with vaulting. I did a handspring full twist and got a 9.45.

On the bars I fell off on my kip catch because I did the trick wrong. I didn't get my hips high enough, and I let go of the low bar too early. But I did make my dismount—a front sole circle back somie, which Olga Korbut introduced in the 1972 Olympics.

On the beam I started with a press handstand mount. My best tricks were a side aerial and a back handspring.

At the end I did a handstand into a handstand double stag. And as my dismount, I did a tucked gainer off the side.

Heather and Ritchey were wonderful on the beam.

Ginny did her back somie and didn't fall off. She was the only one in the meet who did that trick.

The German girls had more dance and fewer tricks in their routines.

Floor was last. Eve and Susan were the first two girls to go, and both of them did the best they've ever done.

While the judges were figuring out the scores, we exhibited our group sequence.

Then they gave out the prizes. Our team won! They gave us certificates in German.

When the meet was over, we exchanged presents with the members of the two other teams. We gave them all T-shirts. The team from Lüneburg gave us little bags of their famous salt for good luck, and the Rendsburg team gave us patches with their emblem on them.

That night we had a big cookout with the Rendsburg team and all our German families. We had knockwursts, which look like big hot dogs, and Holger and Annette drank a lot of beer.

We taught the Germans to play duck duck goose and leap frog.

The next morning we went to the town hall to visit the Senator of Culture. He told us that the town of Rendsburg was over eight hundred years old and that it had been a Danish fortress in 1850. He had a special party for us and gave us each a souvenir plate and a little pin showing Rendsburg's coat of arms. We gave him a bouquet of flowers.

Afterwards we went shopping at Adidas for leotards.

The next day we all got on a special bus and went sightseeing. When we stopped for lunch, we saw a chimney sweeper. You're supposed to have good luck if you touch him. He let me try on his hat.

We also went to the North Sea, which is so cold you turn blue.

Since the sea was so cold, we went swimming nearby in the neatest pool I've ever seen! There was a special machine that made big waves every half-hour for ten minutes. It was just like swimming in the ocean except we didn't freeze to death.

The only bad thing was that we had to wear bathing caps. Even the men are supposed to wear them.

Soon it was time to say goodbye. All our German families came to the station to see us off. Karin and I promised to write each other. I hope she can come and visit me sometime in New York.

We went on by train to Stuttgart and Radolfzell for two more meets before returning to New York. Our whole trip lasted two weeks, and then it was time to fly home. I was sorry to leave but excited to get back because I was looking forward to gym camp.

This summer I didn't go to gym camp until August, so during July I worked on my diving. I take lessons with Carl Samuelson, who is the swimming coach at Williams College during the winter. We usually start on the low board, working on my approach. That's the most important part, because if you have a bad approach it throws off your whole dive. Then I work on basic dives and use of the board.

Diving helps a lot with gymnastics because it all relates to body control. The main difference is in controlling your center of gravity. In gymnastics it moves forward at a faster rate because you're moving so fast. In diving it moves more slowly and is more controlled, so this is good practice. Another way diving helps me is by keeping me in shape when I'm not doing gymnastics.

I like working on the high board. What I like best of all are flips, especially back flip layouts. Olympic divers usually do triples, but I can only do a single. I haven't even tried a double.

Diving is fun, but I love gymnastics much more. Diving is too cold. I'm always freezing. It's torture!

This summer I went to Muriel Grossfeld's camp for one week. It's at Hobart College in upstate New York.

On the first night we were welcomed by the staff and introduced to five Elite gymnasts who train at Muriel's school in Connecticut. The Elite division is made up of the best gymnasts from all over the United States, and our teams for the Olympics, the World Games, and the Pan American Games are usually chosen from this group.

After the introductions, we had a screening session. They made us do twenty pushups and things like that, and we had to perform in all four events. They told us not to be nervous—that we weren't competing in the Olympics. They just wanted to see what level we were best suited for.

 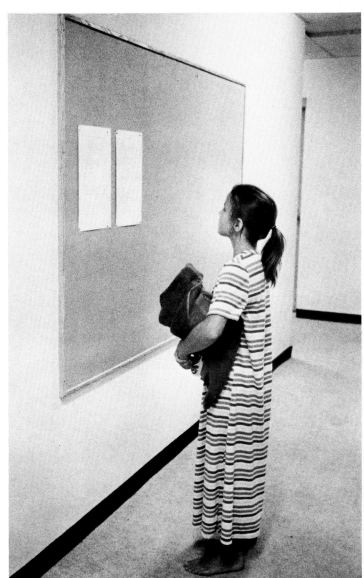

Annette came to camp with me because they have special workshops for coaches. We all had roommates, and mine was Bryn Fenton. After the testing was over, Annette, Bryn, and I went over our score cards together. That night, before we went to bed, they posted the results and the daily schedule on the bulletin boards in our dormitories. I was assigned to Level V, the most advanced group.

Each day started with warmups at 8:45 a.m. in the gym. Leslie Russo and Lisa Shirk, two of the Elite gymnasts, were in charge. They are so strong. When they're in training, they push cars up and down hills to develop their muscles.

We warmed up for fifteen to twenty minutes and had to do many more exercises than we do in our team practice. Annette told me to pay attention so I could lead warmups at school in the fall.

My group started each day with tumbling. Mostly I worked with a coach named Joe Litow on getting more height to my somie in a tuck position. To do a good somie, you need a good spring off the mat.

We had a dance class too. We did ballet and modern dance and worked on glissades and assemblés—movements that are in our beam compulsory.

Our teacher, Pat Panichas, told us that dance isn't just the body—it's the brain too. When we skipped across the floor, she said we should think of our hip bones as two little headlights of a car facing forward.

We worked on vaulting in two stages. For the first few days we concentrated on our pre-flight, with a vaulting board and a crash mat. I had to pretend that the horse was there and that I was vaulting over it.

Then we worked on the after-flight, from the trampoline. This time we used the horse, and Michael Hicks spotted us to make sure we had a good landing and rebound. We don't have a trampoline at school, so this was fun.

Every afternoon we worked with Don Peters on advanced somersaults. Don is Muriel's main teacher. He's one of the best technicians in this country and the head coach for the Elite Team. He had three gymnasts at the Olympic trials in 1976 and seven Elite gymnasts this year.

We practiced doing front layout full twists. First you stand on the horse and jump on to the mini-tramp. As you're coming off the mini-tramp, it's important to get a straight, high jump. Then you wrap one arm across your body, which makes you twist in a layout position. You're supposed to land standing up on the foam rubber mats, but we weren't always that lucky. I had never done this before.

Don also taught us to do a front somie pike, which is easier because our bodies don't have to be so fully extended.

Later that day I won a prize for being the first one to do a front layout full twist the correct way. Don pinned a blue ribbon on me.

He also taught us bars. He had made a floor bar from a broken uneven parallel bar, which is a great idea because it's less scary when you're learning new tricks. I practiced my handstand pirouette, trying to get my grips right. I concentrated on my form too—on keeping my body straight and tight.

When Don worked with us, we used a single bar. He showed me how to do a straight body cast to a handstand. He told me to keep my head down a little more and hollow out, which means stomach in, seat down and under, and your body in a straight line. You should feel like there's nothing inside you.

On beam we worked a lot with Leslie Russo. She demonstrated a special kind of handspring—like Nadia's—for us. Then we all tried to do it. You have to go up very high and split early. My legs always split a little late.

I really liked working with Leslie, so I usually practiced with her in my free workout periods. She's my idol, and I hope to be on the National Team someday the way she is.

One of my best friends was Bali. We practiced a lot together and also played a lot of Ping-Pong during our free time. We would rally, and once we made it up to 251 without missing. There usually wasn't that much free time though.

On the last day of camp Muriel Grossfeld came and worked with each group. She worked on beam with us. When she was little she used to be an acrobat, and she was on the U.S. Olympic Team three times.

She told me to think of my arms as isolated from my body. When I do a turn or a leap, I should think of my upper body as a passenger and let my legs do the work. She said if I am doing this, I should be able to clean my ears while I leap.

Muriel told us that the whole key to success on the beam is to be on balance. The reason Nadia looks so good on beam is that her hips are always square and her shoulders are always centered. Muriel said we should feel like one of those roly-poly dolls with a weight on the bottom.

Working with Muriel was such an inspiration to me. She said that when she was my age she already knew she wanted to make the Olympics, and that even though she wasn't the greatest gymnast when she was little, she never gave up working toward that goal. But I'm not sure if I really want to push myself that far. It might mean moving away from home to train full time, and I think I'd miss Mom and Clifton too much. And my friends too. Anyway, that's all in the future.

Right now what I really want is to get my back layout on the beam and make it stick.

Acknowledgments

Finding Torrance was easy. I first heard about her from Leigh Welles, her ballet teacher, during the summer of 1976 while I was working on *A Very Young Rider*. And then it seemed that whenever I mentioned I was looking for a "very young" gymnast, the name Torrance York came up. I finally telephoned her and we made plans to meet at her apartment the following night. And I have to say, the minute she walked into the room my heart did a flip: I knew she was perfect.

I started out knowing very little about gymnastics and everyone was always eager to help me, especially Annette and Holger Asmus. I'm also indebted to Torrance's teammates for letting me share a year of workouts and competitions with them—plus a week in Germany. I wish now that they hadn't shared quite so much with me—namely their candy and bubble gum *after* those workouts and competitions. I am pleased, however, to report that after a year and a half of practicing under Torrance's often exasperated coaching, I can now blow a perfect bubble-within-a-bubble.

I would also like to thank the staff and students at Muriel Grossfeld's summer camp for letting me be part of that week with them. I can't say I was crazy about the daily room inspections at seven a.m., but I probably learned more about gymnastics during those seven days than at any other time. I even got to try a few things myself—like a dip step on the balance beam. Joan Hicks, Don Peters, Claudia Catalano, and the members of the Elite Team were particularly helpful.

Another person who deserves very special thanks is Cathy Rigby, who took time out of a busy schedule to read over the finished manuscript and check the final layout. Her suggestions were invaluable. It will be hard for me ever to forget the image of her demonstrating a particular tumbling pass across the floor of her hotel room at six one morning. That was the hour she had suggested we meet so that she could catch a nine o'clock plane back to California.

Marilyn Cross and Linda Chenanski, who are both top gymnastics judges, also went over the manuscript and helped me with many technicalities. So did Frank Bare, who is the Executive Director of the U.S. Gymnastics Federation. Michael Burke paved the way for me to cover all those special events at Madison Square Garden. Cheryl Rossum and Ed Buchbinder loaned me special camera equipment and, even more importantly, showed me how to use it.

A big thank you to my assistants June Makela and Heidi Steinberger. Also, to my friend Kurt Vonnegut, who was a part of this project from beginning to end.

As with *A Very Young Dancer* and *A Very Young Rider,* this book has been a truly collaborative endeavor with the gang at Alfred A. Knopf. My editor, Bob Gottlieb, was his usual brilliant self; Bob Scudellari and Elissa Ichiyasu worked on the final layout and design; Neal Jones and Becky Mlynarczyk did the copy editing; Teddy Slater and Joyce Portnoy did the proofreading; Marylea O'Reilly steered it through the final production stages; and Martha Kaplan, Chuck Elliott, Jane Friedman, Maria Temechko, Nina Bourne, and Karen Latuchie offered good advice and encouragement along the way. I would also like to take this opportunity to thank Fabio Coen, Pat Ross, Carole Ouziel, Kathy Wisch, and Sophie Silberberg, all of whom are part of Knopf's juvenile department, for everything they have done on behalf of these "Very Young" books. I feel so lucky to be part of such a wonderful publishing house. I can't imagine being anywhere else.

In closing I would like to thank the York family—Torrance, Clifton, and Janet—for being absolutely wonderful every minute along the way. And there's one more thing you should know: Torrance qualified for the A.A.U. Junior Olympics just as this book was going to press!

—Jill Krementz

A Note About the Author

Jill Krementz is a well-known photographer of literary figures, a documentary photographer, and an author. Her pictures can be seen regularly in the *New York Times*, *New York* magazine, *People*, *Newsweek*, and other major periodicals, and she has photographs in the permanent collections of the Museum of Modern Art, the Delaware Art Museum, and the Library of Congress. Her previous books are *The Face of South Vietnam*, with Dean Brelis; *Sweet Pea — A Black Girl Growing Up in the Rural South; Words and Their Masters*, with Israel Shenker; *A Very Young Dancer;* and *A Very Young Rider.*

A Note on the Type

This book was set in a film version of Bulmer, a distinguished typeface long famous in the history of English printing, which was designed and cut by William Martin in about 1790 for William Bulmer of the Shakespeare Press. In design, it is all but a modern face, with vertical stress, sharp differentiation between the thick and thin strokes, and nearly flat serifs. The italic is taken from a font of Baskerville; Martin was John Baskerville's pupil.

The book was composed by Quad Typographers, Inc., New York, New York. It was printed by Halliday Lithographers, West Hanover, Massachusetts, and bound by American Book-Stratford Press, Saddle Brook, New Jersey.

Graphics were directed by R. D. Scudellari; book design and layout by Elissa Ichiyasu.

DATE DUE

DEC 9 '80			
APR 28 '83			
OCT 7 '85			
OCT 11 '86			
GAYLORD			PRINTED IN U.S A